SING A SONG FOR FU

Mary Martin and Valerie Stumbles

Illustrated by Helen Stanton

CASSELL

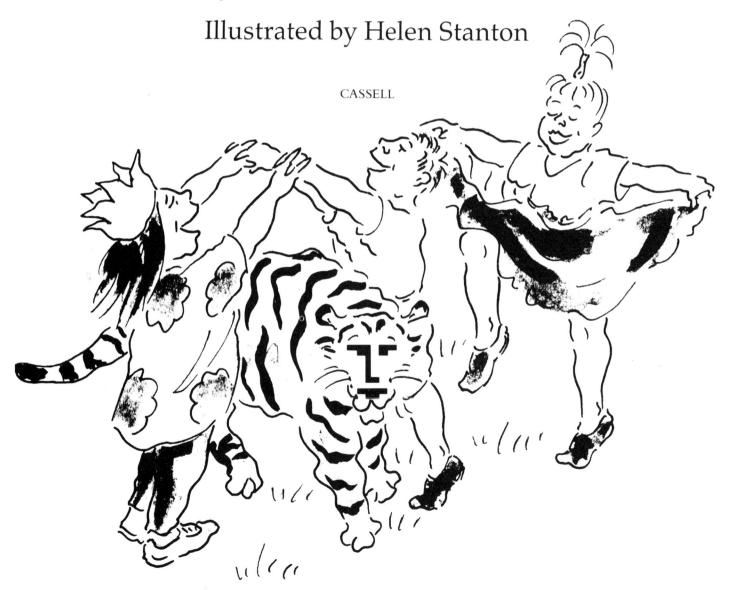

CONTENTS

PREFACE

THE COLLECTION of songs within this book is a complete mixture of inspiration and perspiration! Within the classroom there were topics which sparked off lyrics and tunes, and there were other topics which needed lyrics and tunes to spark them off. Whichever way they came about, they have all proved to be of some use in the classroom environment, and are enjoyed by the children as a source of musical fun.

They have been divided into four categories: Numbers, The Year, People, and Imagination. All the songs are intended to be sung any time, anywhere and for any reason, but there are more serious undertones.

Each song can be treated as part of a topic, and for that reason we have attempted to categorize the songs under the National Curriculum attainment targets wherever possible. Although the music curriculum is as yet unpublished, we are sure that it will contain elements that are basic to all education: listening skills, sense of rhythm, pitch, etc., all are practised whilst using these songs for fun.

We hope that your children have as much fun singing these songs as ours did!

Mary Martin and Valerie Stumbles
West Rise Infant School, Eastbourne

The following abbreviations are used:

CDT   Craft, design and technology
EA   English attainment
MA   Maths attainment
ScA   Science attainment

NUMBERS

ALL THESE SONGS keep the number count within ten. They are all gentle reminders of counting in ones and twos, odd or even, backwards or forwards.

Each song can easily be dramatized for small children and could provide a centrepiece for a class assembly or similar gathering.

Once learned, the children can use the songs as props for further mathematical work.

Mrs Odd   MA 2, 3
The Even Numbers   MA 2, 3
Count to Ten   MA 2, 3
Ten Little Chickens   MA 2, 3

MRS ODD

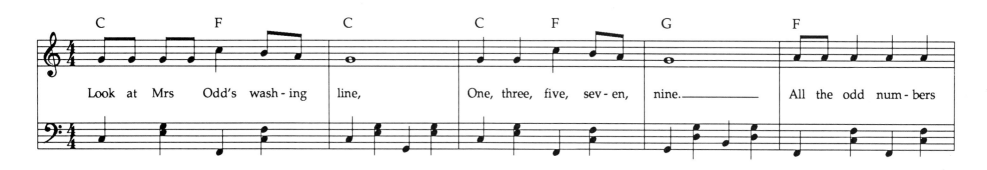

Look at Mrs Odd's wash-ing line, One, three, five, sev - en, nine._____ All the odd num - bers

hang-ing in a row, All the odd num - bers wav-ing to and fro. One, three, five, sev - en, nine._____

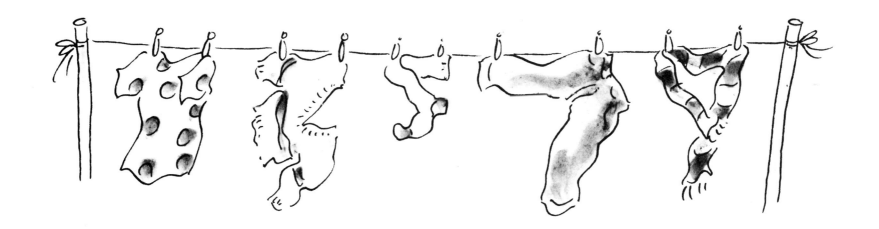

THE EVEN NUMBERS

Down in the hen-house sits mo-ther hen, Coun-ting her eggs, two, four, six, eight, ten.

Wait-ing for the day they will hatch and then They'll all be flu-ffy chicks, two, four, six, eight, ten.

COUNT TO TEN

I can count to ten on my hands so ea-si-ly, ea-si-ly, ea-si-ly, I can count to ten on my hands so ea-si-ly, I'll show what I can do.

v. 1. There are five here and now I need five more. There are six here so now I need just four.
v. 2. There are seven here and now I need just three. There are eight here and two more now I see.
v. 3. There are nine here and now I need just one. There are ten here so no more just for fun.
} I can

TEN LITTLE CHICKENS

v. 1. Farmer Brown had ten little chickens. Ten little chickens had Farmer Brown. Farmer Brown had ten little chickens Till one little chicken fell down, fell down, Till one little chicken fell down.

v. 2. Farmer Brown had nine little chickens.
Nine little chickens had Farmer Brown.
Farmer Brown had nine little chickens
Till one little chicken fell down, fell down,
Till one little chicken fell down.

etc.

Last verse:

Farmer Brown had no little chickens.
No little chickens had Farmer Brown.
Farmer Brown had no little chickens
So then Farmer Brown went to town, went to town,
So then Farmer Brown went to town.

THE YEAR

THIS COLLECTION of songs would seem to be inappropriately categorized. However, it proved very difficult to consider them in any other light as they have been used right from January through to December at various events.

Quite a few of these songs provide children with the opportunity to take hold of the musical instruments available in school and play along.

THE MONTHS

THE WEATHER

I heard the wea-ther man say, It's a rai-ny, rai-ny day. I need my old um-

brell-a to-day. It's a rai-ny, rai-ny day. *Fine* What-ev-er the wea-ther,

Whe-ther it rains or shines. What-ev-er the wea-ther, Eve-ry-thing will turn out fine.

FESTIVAL

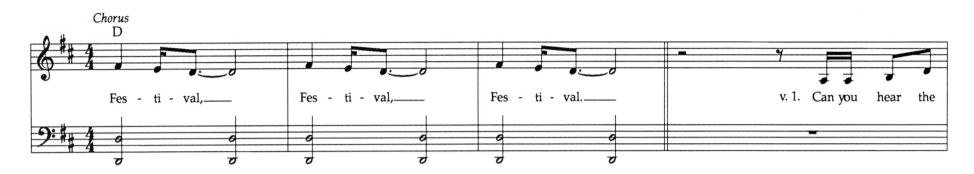

Chorus

Fes - ti - val,_____ Fes - ti - val,_____ Fes - ti - val._____ v. 1. Can you hear the

sound_____ of chil-dren sing - ing?____ Can you feel the joy_____ that they are bring - ing?_____ Can you join their

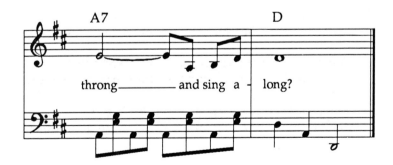

throng_____ and sing a - long?

v. 2. Can you feel the fun of children playing?
Can you feel the joy that they are making?
Can you join their throng and sing along?

v. 3. Can you see the sight of children giving?
Can you feel the joy when they're receiving?
Can you join their throng and sing along?

WHAT WE NEED IS RHYTHM

What we need is rhy - thm. What we need is beat. What we need is mu - sic so we can tap our feet.

v. 1. Some - one click your fin - gers. Keep a stea - dy beat. Join in with a chime bar and keep the sound quite sweet.

What we have is rhy - thm, mu - sic loud and clear. Come and join our cho - rus, our Fes - ti - val is here.

v. 2.   Someone slap your legs and keep a steady beat.
         Join in with a chime bar and keep the sound quite sweet.

v. 3.   Someone clap your hands and keep a steady beat.
         Join in with a chime bar and keep the sound quite sweet.

v. 4.   Someone tap your feet and keep a steady beat.
         Join in with a chime bar and keep the sound quite sweet.

EASTER SWEETS

MUMMY, IT'S COLD OUTSIDE

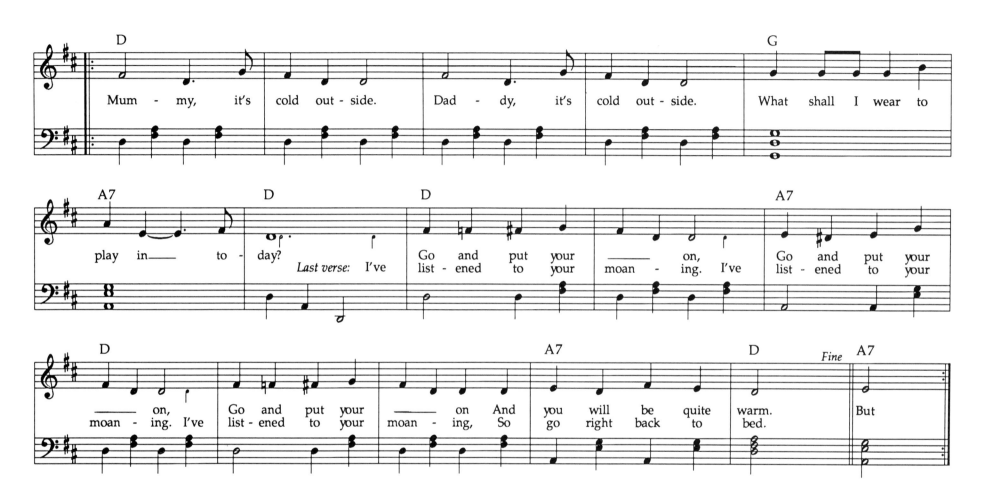

Repeat the verse, using a different garment each time.
When the child is 'dressed', or you are fed up, sing the last verse.

THE SCARECROW

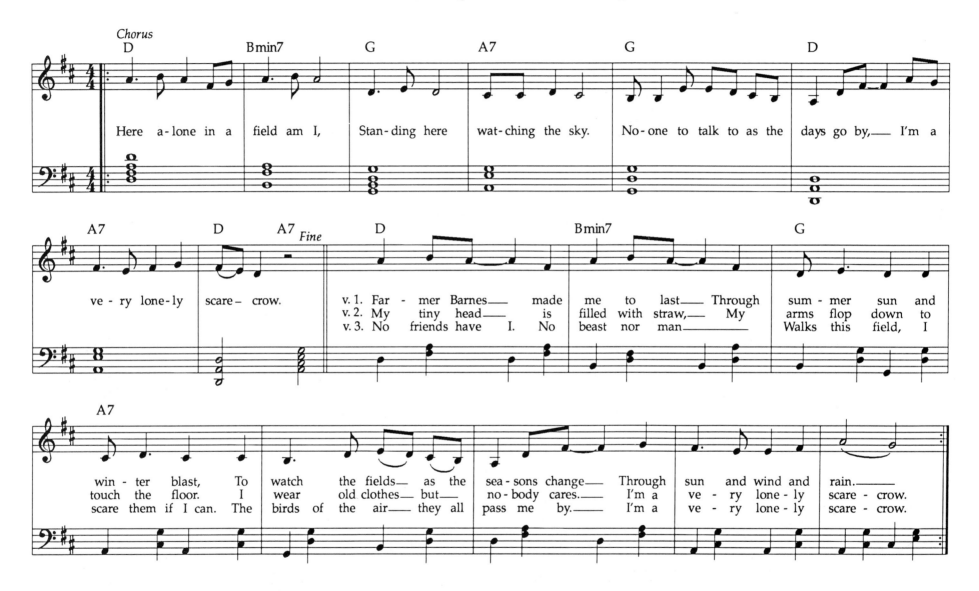

Here a-lone in a field am I, Stan-ding here wat-ching the sky. No-one to talk to as the days go by,— I'm a

ve-ry lone-ly scare-crow.

v. 1. Far - mer Barnes— made me to last— Through sum - mer sun and
v. 2. My tiny head— is filled with straw,— My arms flop down to
v. 3. No friends have I. No beast nor man— Walks this field, I

win - ter blast, To watch the fields— as the sea-sons change— Through sun and wind and rain.— I'm a ve - ry lone - ly scare-crow.
touch the floor. I wear old clothes— but no-body cares. I'm a ve - ry lone - ly scare-crow.
scare them if I can. The birds of the air— they all pass me by.— I'm a ve - ry lone-ly scare-crow.

THE RAINBOW

PEOPLE

ONCE AGAIN, all these songs came about because of a need within the classroom to get a message across. Much talk on the subject of strangers has never really got the message home conclusively, yet the children readily sang the song and learned to shout 'NO' most emphatically in no time at all.

Happy events such as the birth of a baby brother or sister are always celebrated at school but there seemed to be a lack of a 'birthday' song for the new-born.

The remaining two songs in this category rely on the teacher's imagination and ingenuity, but be prepared, they become firm favourites with the children!

Never Go with Strangers   EA 1, 2
I Went to the Market   EA 1, 2
Hey, Can You Tell Me?   EA 1, 2
My Mum's Had a Baby   EA 1, 2. Sc.A 3, 4
Green Cross Code   EA 1, 2

NEVER GO WITH STRANGERS

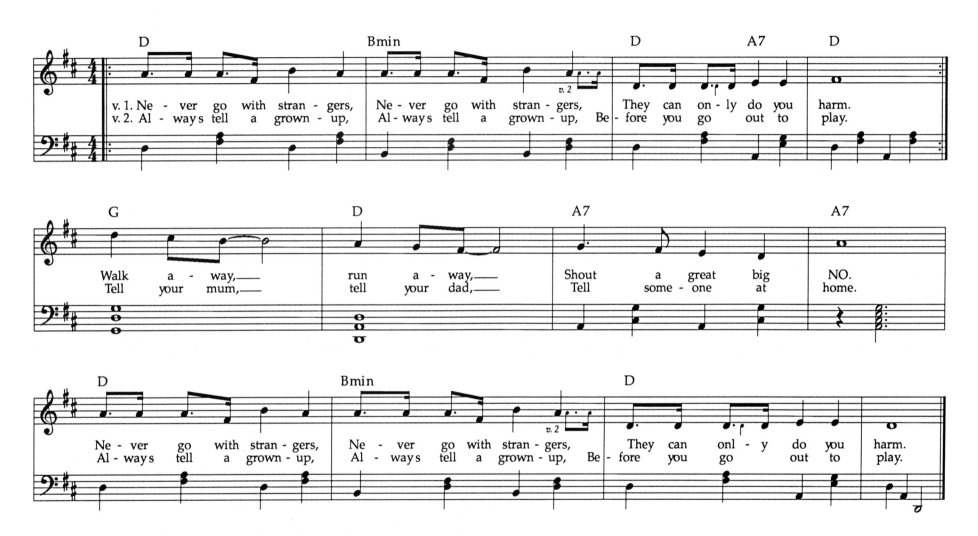

I WENT TO THE MARKET

I went to the mar - ket ___ and what did I buy? ___ I bought an ap - ple and a ba - na - na and a

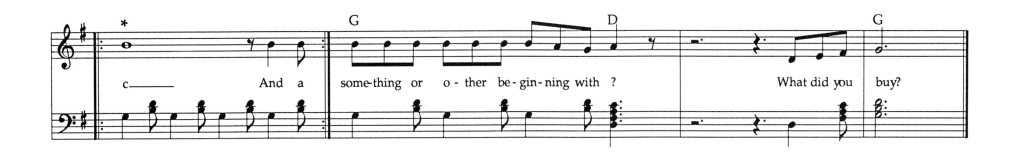

c ___ And a some-thing or o - ther be - gin - ning with ? What did you buy?

Child chooses an item beginning with the next letter of the alphabet.
Decide on the correct rhythm and sing note B at this ∗ point.

HEY, CAN YOU TELL ME?

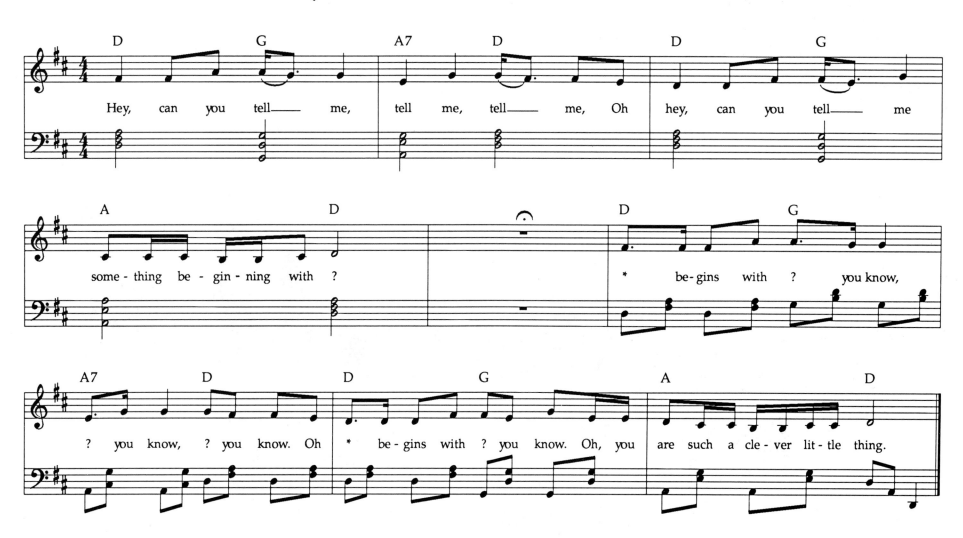

Alternative version for number work

Hey, can you tell me, tell me, tell me,

Oh hey, can you tell me two numbers that make ?

  * and * make ? you know, ? you know, ? you know.

  * and * make ? you know. Oh, you are such a clever little thing.

? substitute initial letter, or sound.

* give word beginning with that letter or sound.

25

MY MUM'S HAD A BABY

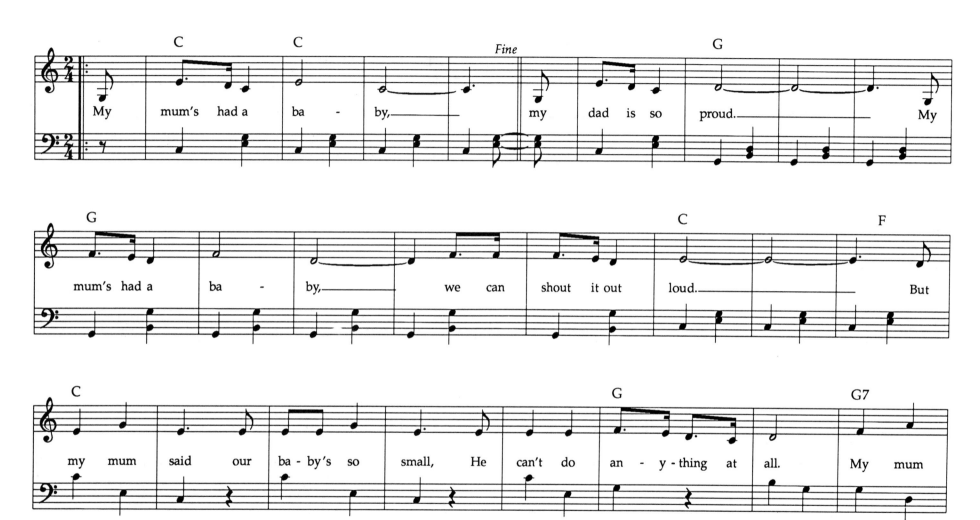

My mum's had a ba - by,_____ my dad is so proud._____ My

mum's had a ba - by,_____ we can shout it out loud._____ But

my mum said our ba - by's so small, He can't do an - y - thing at all. My mum

GREEN CROSS CODE

IMAGINATION

THE FINAL category is truly the most adequately labelled. Each song conjures up a picture that hopefully will allow a child's imagination to take flight. Once again, all the songs can be arranged for percussion accompaniment or dramatization, and each stands on its own or as part of a topic. The range here is from skeletons to cars made of jelly!

The Little Wooden Horse   CDT
A Bundle of Bones   EA2
The Highroad of Song   EA2
Hey, Mr Giraffe   Sc.A2
The Dragon   Sc.A2
In the Malayan Jungle   Sc.A2
Land of Make-Believe   EA2
The Puppets   CDT

THE LITTLE WOODEN HORSE

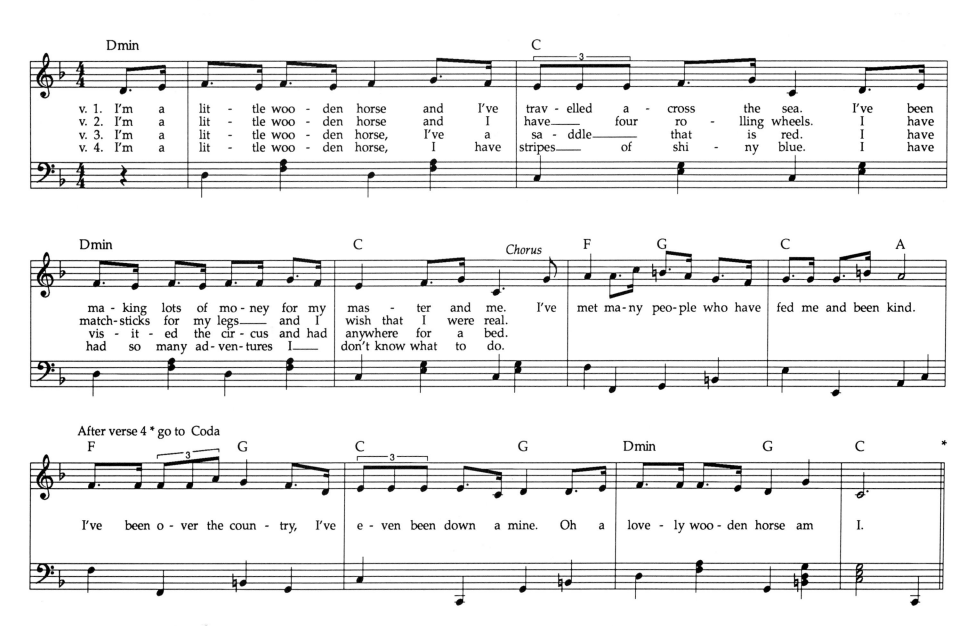

* Coda

I've been o - ver the coun - try but my ma - ster I must find. Oh a love - ly woo - den horse am I.

A BUNDLE OF BONES

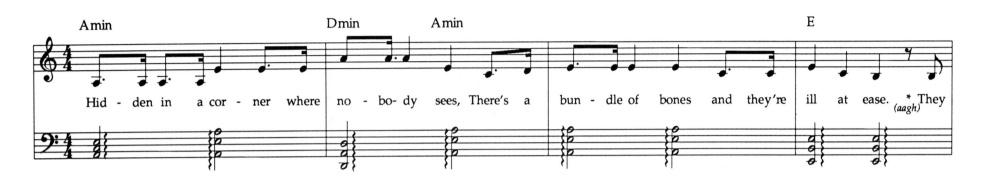

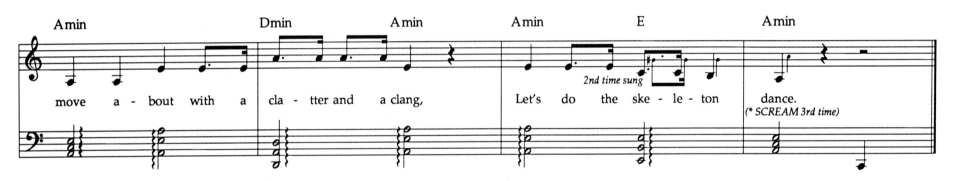

1. Sing.   2. Hum and dance.   3. Sing and scream to end.

THE HIGHROAD OF SONG

HEY, MR GIRAFFE

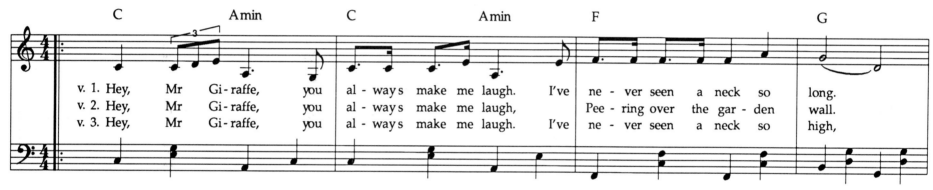

v. 1. Hey, Mr Gi-raffe, you al-ways make me laugh. I've ne-ver seen a neck so long.
v. 2. Hey, Mr Gi-raffe, you al-ways make me laugh, Pee-ring over the gar-den wall.
v. 3. Hey, Mr Gi-raffe, you al-ways make me laugh. I've ne-ver seen a neck so high,

Is it 'cause you're ve-ry strong? I want to know.
Why are you so ve-ry tall?
Rea-ches right up to the sky.

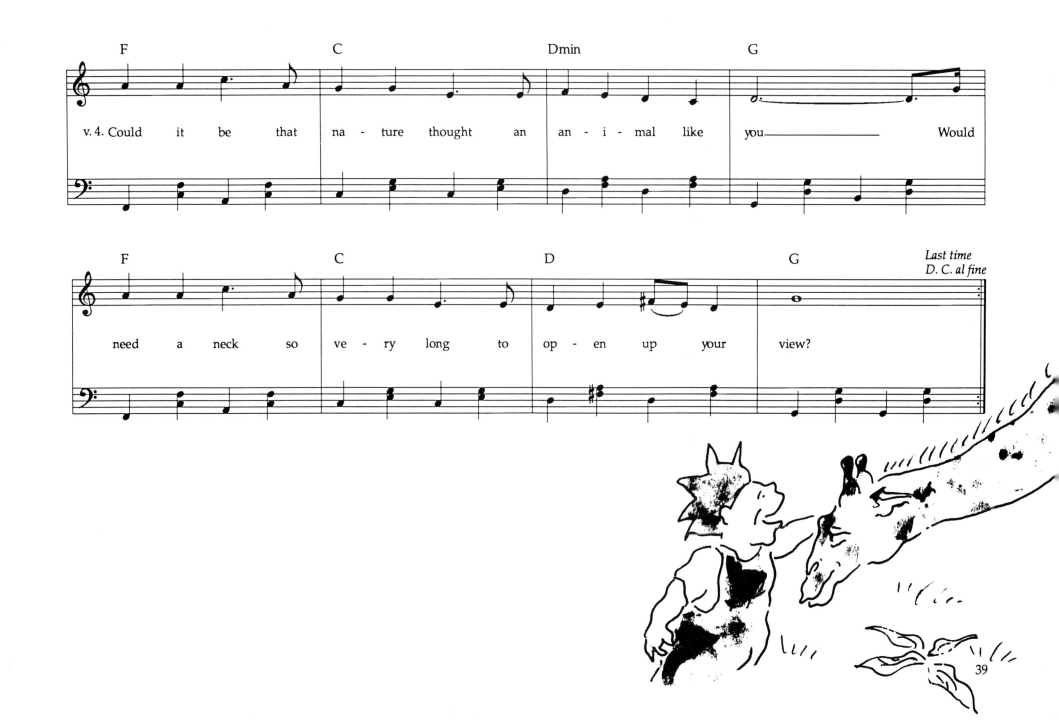

THE DRAGON

1. There once was a dra - gon who breathed fire.___ There once was a dra - gon who breathed fire.___ He liked roast - ing chi - ckens, he liked roast - ing lambs, But most of all___ he___ liked roast - ing hams. Oh a jol - ly fine dra - gon was he.

v. 2. There once was a dragon who cried tears.
There once was a dragon who cried tears.
He cried in the bathroom, he cried on the phone,
But most of all he cried when all alone.
Oh a jolly fine dragon was he.

v. 3. There once was a dragon who would sneeze.
There once was a dragon who would sneeze.
He sneezed in the kitchen, he sneezed in the hall,
But most of all he sneezed whene'er you'd call.
Oh a jolly fine dragon was he.

v. 4. There once was a dragon who would sing.
There once was a dragon who would sing.
He'd sing in the bathtub, he'd sing in the loo,
But most of all he'd like to sing to you.
Oh a jolly fine dragon was he.

IN THE MALAYAN JUNGLE

In the Ma-la-yan jun-gle, in the Ma-la-yan jun-gle, There's a ti-ger black and

yell-ow striped. There's a tig-er with his eyes shin-ing bright.

Prow-ling in the jun-gle, prow-ling in the jun-gle, Wait-ing for a bite.

THE LAND OF MAKE-BELIEVE

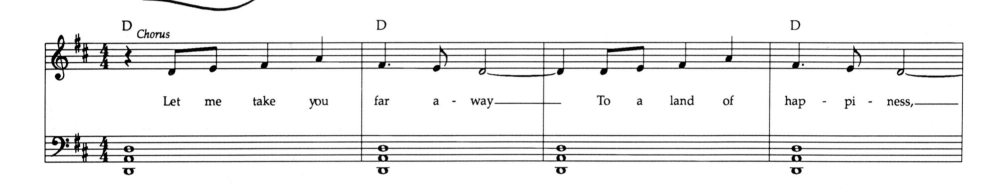

Let me take you far a-way____ To a land of hap - pi - ness,____

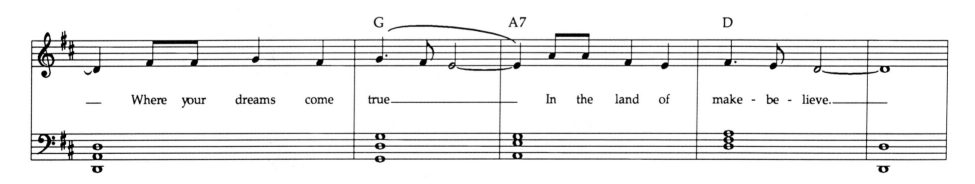

__ Where your dreams come true____ In the land of make - be - lieve.____

v. 1. Choc'-late sol-diers march to and fro___ To guard a su-gar-mouse queen. Trees sit down___ to
v. 2. Teddy-bears ski___ ov-er ice-cream fields___ And candy-floss clouds float by. Jel-ly cars___ they

have a rest___ But make sure they're ne-ver seen In the land of make-be-lieve.
bump and slide___ And so no - one ev-er cries In the land of make-be-lieve

THE PUPPETS

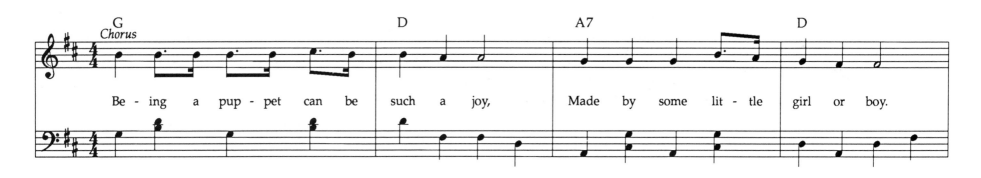

Be - ing a pup - pet can be such a joy, Made by some lit - tle girl or boy.

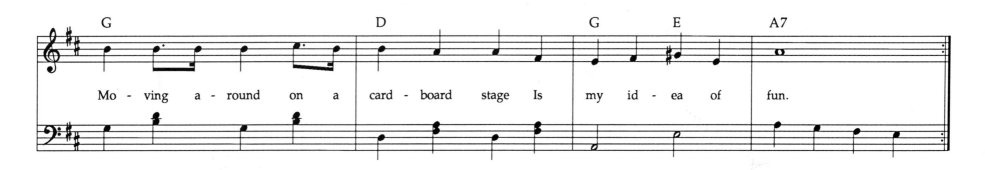

Mo - ving a - round on a card - board stage Is my id - ea of fun.

v. 1. Eve - ry - bo - dy knows I'm just a pup - pet on a string. Eve - ry - bo - dy knows that if I dance or sing, Then

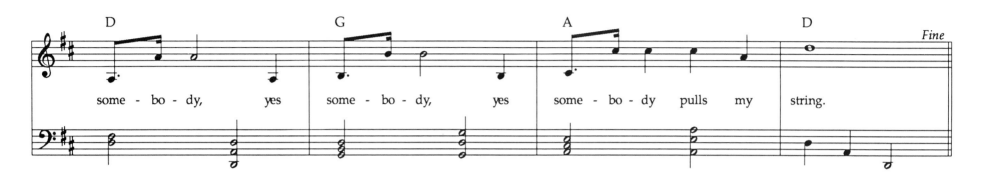

some - bo - dy,   yes   some - bo - dy,   yes   some - bo - dy   pulls   my   string.

v. 2.   Everybody knows I'm just a puppet on a hand.
        Everybody knows that if I sit or stand,
        Then somebody, yes somebody, yes somebody moves their hand.

v. 3.   Everybody knows I'm just a puppet on a stick.
        Everybody knows that if I dance or kick,
        Then somebody, yes somebody, yes somebody moves the stick.

v. 4.   Everybody knows I'm just a shadow on a wall.
        Everybody knows that if I move at all,
        Then somebody, yes somebody, yes somebody works it all.

After last chorus sing verse 1 again to finish at *Fine*.

Cassell Educational Limited,
Villiers House, 41/47 Strand,
London WC2N 5JE

© Cassell Educational Limited 1990

First published 1990

British Library Cataloguing in Publication Data
Martin, Mary, *1949* -
Sing a song for fun.
1. Children's songs in English
I. Title II. Stumbles, Valerie, *1937* -
782.42083

ISBN : 0-304-32320-9

Music and text typeset by Linda Lancaster

Printed and bound in Great Britain by Hollen Street Press Limited, Slough